BENJAMIN BRITTEN

Suite for Harp

Op. 83

Edited by Osian Ellis

1. Overture

2. Toccata

3. Nocturne

4. Fugue

5. Hymn (St. Denio)

The first performance of the *Suite for Harp* was given by
Osian Ellis at the Aldeburgh Festival, 24 June 1969

Duration: 14 minutes

First Published in 1970 by Faber Music Ltd
Bloomsbury House 74–77 Great Russell Street London WC1B 3DA
Cover design by S & M Tucker
Printed in England by Caligraving Ltd
All rights reserved

ISBN10: 0-571-50360-8
EAN13: 978-0-571-50360-5

For Osian

EDITOR'S NOTE

In the first movement the chords must sound resonant and the use of alternating hands is indicated by the composer for this purpose. In the opening bar and the first bar on p. 4 the second of the triplet chords should be played tenuto, lengthening the arpeggio. The first of the two semiquavers (sixteenth notes) which follow—and in similar passages subsequently—should be played faster than usual. (This shortening of note values often occurs in the music of Purcell.)

In the Nocturne the exact patterns of the right-hand tremolando notes should be carefully followed. Note the effect at the end of the movement, where the bottom F must be allowed to reverberate while the previous chord is damped, so that it still sounds even when the final pianissimo chord has died away. It is extremely effective for the Fugue to follow *attacca* without a break.

The composer has carefully marked all the chords or octaves which he wishes to be played *arpeggiando*. The timing of glissandos has also been precisely indicated.

I have shown some of the fingerings that I use. There may be others more convenient to some players. In the Nocturne and parts of the Hymn, I make very little use of the right-hand thumb, since I find that a more *cantabile* quality is achieved by using the other fingers.

If the harp has no bottom C string, bottom D should be tuned to D flat and back to D natural after the Toccata. If the harp has no top G string, top F can be tuned to F sharp— the upward glissando in the first bar of p. 9 will end on E—and before the Hymn the F must be tuned up to G natural.

The left-hand glissandi in the passage starting on the third system of p. 3 can be played as follows:

OSIAN ELLIS

SUITE
for Harp

Edited by Osian Ellis

BENJAMIN BRITTEN
Op. 83

I OVERTURE

4

broadly (like the start)

II TOCCATA

Fast and gay (♩ = 120–126)

III NOCTURNE

IV FUGUE

V HYMN
(St. Denio)

Aldeburgh
March 18th 1969